Copyright © 2020 Andre H.

All rights reserved
No part of this book may be reproduced, or stored in a retrieval system, or transmitted in any form or by any means, electronic, mechanical, photocopying, recording, or otherwise, without express written permission of the publisher.

Unless otherwise noted, all scriptures are from the NEW KING JAMES VERSION®. Copyright© 1982 by Thomas Nelson, Inc. Used by permission. All rights reserved.
Scripture quotations taken from the The Holy Bible, Berean Study Bible, BSB Copyright ©2016, 2018 by Bible Hub
Used by Permission. All Rights Reserved Worldwide.
Scripture quotations from The Authorized (King James) Version. Rights in the Authorized Version in the United Kingdom are vested in the Crown. Reproduced by permission of the Crown's patentee, Cambridge University Press
Scripture quotations taken from the English Standard Version (ESV). Copyright © 2001 by Crossway, a publishing ministry of Good News Publishers. Used by permission. All rights reserved.
Scripture quotations taken from the New American Standard Bible (NASB). Copyright © 1960, 1962, 1963, 1968, 1971, 1972, 1973, 1975, 1977, 1995 by The Lockman Foundation. Used by permission. All rights reserved.
Scripture quotations taken from the HOLY BIBLE, New International Version (NIV). Copyright © 1973, 1978, 1984, 2011 by Biblica, Inc.™. Used by permission. All rights reserved.
Scripture quotations taken from the New Living Translation (NLT). Copyright © 1996, 2004, 2007 by Tyndale House Foundation. Used by permission. All rights reserved.
Scripture quotations marked HCSB are taken from the Holman Christian Standard Bible®, Used by Permission HCSB ©1999,2000,2002,2003,2009 Holman Bible Publishers. Holman Christian Standard Bible®, Holman CSB®, and HCSB® are federally registered trademarks of Holman Bible Publishers

Cover design picture by: https://pixabay.com/illustrations/phoenix-bird-fire-sun-bright-red-500469/ (Material not copy righted)

CONTENTS

Introduction
The Struggle is Real
  Five Dimensions of Our Lives
  Choose Life
  Jesus, the Abundant Life-Giver
  Jesus' Earthly Ministry Defined
Spiritual Dimension
  Man: Made in God's Image and Likeness
  What Does God "Look" Like?
  Separated from God: Lost Relationship with God
  Reconciled to God: Regaining Our Spiritual Relationship to God
  The Holy Spirit: The Supernatural Gift to Mankind
  The Holy Spirit: My Guide in Coming to America (USA)
  The Holy Spirit: My Comforter
Emotional Dimension
  <u>Spiritually Restored With a Broken Heart</u>
  He Came to Heal the Brokenhearted
  Keys to Start the Healing Process
    Love: The Healing Balm
    Believe and Receive Healing
    Forgive Those Who've Sinned and Will Sin Against You
    Forgive Yourself.

- Mental Dimension
  - <u>God's Gift: Peaceful and Sound Minds</u>
    - He is Our Peace
    - God Gave Us a Sound Mind
  - Keep Your Mind Focused on God and His Word
  - Proclaim God's Word Concerning His Promises
  - Be anxious for nothing
  - Don't Carry Your Burdens by Yourself
  - Renewing Our Minds
  - Expel the Unfruitful Works of Darkness
    - Destroy Thoughts Contrary to God's Word
    - Love God with Your Mind/Intellect
- Physical Dimension
  - He is the God Who Heals Us (Jehovah Rapha)
  - It is God's Will to Heal People
  - God Has Healed Me and Others
  - The Gospel Includes The Good News of God as Our Healer
  - By His Stripes, I am Healed
  - Turn From Evil and Sin No More
- Financial Dimension
  - Money Does Matter to God
  - Money is a Matter of Our Hearts
  - God Will Provide for You
    - <u>Childlike Faith in South Africa</u>
    - God Comes Through Again in the USA
  - Financial Abundance is God's Idea
  - Financial Abundance: God's Covenant Promise
  - Blessed to be a Blessing to the World
  - God's Part and Our Part in Financial Abundance
    - Be Shrewd about Money (Use Wisdom)

    Follow the Holy Spirit for Your Financial Wellbeing
    Follow the Word of God Regarding Your Finances
    Tithes and Offerings
  Final Thoughts Regarding Finances
Your Turn
Final Words
About the Author

INTRODUCTION

"The thief comes only to steal and kill and destroy; I came that they may have life, and have it abundantly. John 10:10 NASB

This book is in part my testimony and a testimony of the goodness of the God that I serve. Why did I write this book? I felt God dealing with me for a considerable amount of time to put in writing what He has done for me and what He has taught me. I had no idea how or where to begin or what to put into the book. However, what I felt strongly impressed in my heart was the fact that so many of God's children do not fully understand what God did for us through Jesus Christ.

When I looked at my life, at the time of writing the book, I recognized how much it has changed since I started serving God. I saw the areas of my life He restored and how faithful He is to His Word. He has truly become my good shepherd who has left me wanting nothing, led me beside still waters, and restored my soul. My cup is running over with the goodness and the mercy of a loving God. He sent Heaven down to Earth to show His love for a fallen and broken humanity. And to think I wanted nothing to do with the Gospel of Jesus Christ for a good part of my life. Even though I rejected Him, He never stopped pursuing me through people and circumstances. He came to seek and save those who are lost, and He never rejected me, but gently pursued me, and eventually won my heart.

So to this end, I put my testimony in writing, that I might bring glory and honour to His name, and that I might help others fully embrace the completed work of the cross of Jesus Christ. I am still learning and discovering the riches of the glory of my inheritance in His holy people. I forget the things that are behind me and reach for those things that are ahead.

So, as you read this book, I pray God will speak to you and that He will leave no broken part of your life untouched. I pray He restores your soul and that He leads you beside still waters, as He did for me.

THE STRUGGLE IS REAL

For our struggle is not against flesh and blood, but against the rulers, against the authorities, against the powers of this dark world and against the spiritual forces of evil in the heavenly realms. Ephesians 6:12 NIV

The struggle for true freedom and abundant life has been a dilemma and struggle for humanity since the dawn of time. We have toiled under the heavy burden of tyranny, war, enslavement, poverty, sickness, and diseases throughout our history. Millions of lives, resources, and money were given and lost to find this elusive freedom. However, the heart and soul of most of us have remained bound and imprisoned by an unseen force that is beyond our ability to control, understand, and overcome. It is a relentless force with no mercy or kindness. It kills, steals, and destroys at will, without regard for human stature, position, or wealth. This force has gone unchecked and almost unrestrained for much of humanity's existence.

There is a silent cry that goes out of our hearts for freedom and abundance. The knowledge and desire to be free is written indelibly on our hearts. It echoes in our heart and screams in our minds: *"There has to be more than this thing called life and human existence."* As a result, many attempts to answer this cry, but all have failed.

We tried to silence that cry with pleasure, wealth, food, drugs, alcohol, religion, and whatever else we could find, but the emptiness in our hearts has only gotten bigger. The more we gained in material wealth, the emptier and less meaningful life became. The cry in the heart of man has only become louder and more desperate.

In the fulness of time, God (the only true and living God) launched a plan of action; He had prepared since the beginning of time. His plan would answer the desperate cry of humanity for freedom, joy, peace, and fulfilment and would give man the meaning for the life he so desperately seeks. God's response was a tremendous and powerful one. It left no doubt that He was "desperate" to answer the cry that emanated from the heart of His creation. In His infinite wisdom and knowledge, He sacrificed something He held precious and dear. Men are still amazed at the great length God went to show His love and concern for them.

Whether you embrace God or reject Him, whether you embrace or reject God's answer, is entirely up to you. To embrace it will change your life forever. If you reject it as I did for so many years, you will be left empty and without meaning and purpose in this thing called life, just like I was. My prayer and most significant desire for you is that you would embrace it and embark on a journey that will leave you breathless and exuberant. Embracing God's answer will open your spiritual eyes, and you will begin to see things happen in your life that you've never dreamed possible. You will find a God who is unconditionally loving, infinitely patient, wonderfully kind, and plentiful in mercy. You will find a God who will fill you with love, joy and peace; a God who will give you so much more than you could ever give to Him in return.

What was God's answer? It was the sacrifice of His only begotten Son, Jesus Christ, who was nailed and hung on a cross (crucified) for humanity. Jesus' ultimate death on a cross was the answer to the desperate cry in the hearts of all of humanity: the desperate cry for unconditional love and acceptance, the cry for meaning and purpose, the cry for peace and joy, and the cry for healing and restoration. The ancient call that has been in the heart of man finally had an answer, and what an answer it was!

God's work on the cross at Calvary, through Jesus, was a complete work that needed nothing added to or taken away from it (John 19:16-42). When Jesus uttered these words on the cross, "It is finished" (John 19:30), He declared victory for all of humanity. Jesus started the restoration of what humanity lost when it fell (Genesis 3). *"It is finished"* began a brand new era in the history and existence of the human race, for those who embrace this truth.

When Jesus purchased our salvation, His sacrifice redeemed every aspect of our lives. His work on the cross is complete. Not one area in our lives is left untouched by the accomplishment of the cross. However; many blood-bought children of God live bound and lacking in their lives, separated from what Jesus paid for with His life. Many still live bound and broken when it was never God's intent for them to remain that way.

When Jesus redeemed us (Galatians 3:13, Revelation 5:9), He not only redeemed us from the curse of sin, He freed us from lack (deficiency) in our *spirit, mind, emotions, physical body, and finances.* He demonstrated His mastery over every aspect of our human existence, as recorded in the Holy Bible.

Let us explore these five areas (dimensions) and how the power of the blood of Jesus Christ bought us victory and freedom.

Five Dimensions Of Our Lives

Now may the God of peace make you holy in every way, and may your whole spirit and soul and body be kept blameless until our Lord Jesus Christ comes again. 1 Thessalonians 5:23 NLT

Let us consider five dimensions/areas of our lives that I believe are significant in terms of living a life that is full of joy, lasting peace, and happiness. I have separated these dimensions/areas into five categories because they are simple to remember, and most of us can quickly identify with these categories: *Spiritual, Emotional, Mental, Physical, and Financial.*

Every one of these areas is significant, and when we lack in any one of these areas, it becomes a stumbling block and hindrance that may result in us not fully living out what God has intended for us. It is not to say that we cannot have great results in some areas of our lives when we lack one or more of these areas. I know many people who had tremendous success in one or more of these areas, but lacked severely in others and as a result, only achieved partial success in their lives overall.

Consider the wealthy sports person or corporate executive who has been successful financially, but lacked (suffered) in their emotional (relationship) life. Maybe they lost their spouse and family in the process of gaining wealth due to the demands and stresses of their business or career. Perhaps they suffered the physical dimension (body) due to lack of rest and exercise. Consider a minister of the Gospel, who spends a considerable part of their time ministering to others, but loses their children or spouse due to neglect. Maybe this minister has tremendous success in the pulpit, but neglects their finances or health, just to suffer the consequences of this neglect. The list is long of people who have paid the price for focusing on only one or two of these areas of their lives. This imbalance leads to shipwrecked lives, theirs and the ones closest to them. All of these areas are important, and each of them requires our time, energy, effort, and attention for us to thrive as healthy human beings.

Choose Life

Now choose life, so that you and your children may live and that you may love the Lord your God, listen to his voice, and hold fast to him. Deuteronomy 30:19 (NIV)

We have to learn to live wisely and make wise choices for every dimension of our lives. God said to the children of Israel, and us today: *"Choose life."*

See, I set before you today *life and prosperity, death and destruction.* For I command you today to love the Lord your God, to walk in obedience to him, and to keep his commands, decrees and laws; then you will live and increase, and the Lord your God will bless you in the land you are entering to possess.
Deuteronomy 30:15-16 (NIV)

This day I call the heavens and the earth as witnesses against you that I have set before you life and death, blessings and curses. *Now choose life,* so that you and your children may live and that you may love the Lord your God, listen to his voice, and hold fast to him. For the Lord is your life, and he will give you many years in the land he swore to give to your fathers, Abraham, Isaac and Jacob.
Deuteronomy 30:19-20 (NIV)

God is saying we should choose life and prosperity, but it also means we can choose death and destruction. We so often choose death and destruction without realizing it, but the results we obtain in our lives are a direct result of our decisions. It is within our power and ability to choose life and prosperity; otherwise, God would not have told us to *"choose."*

Jesus, The Abundant Life-Giver

I have come that they may have life, and that they may have it more abundantly. John 10:10 NKJV

It is not God's intention for us to lack in any one of these five dimensions of our life. Jesus said so much when He said:

All who ever came before me are thieves and robbers, but the sheep did not hear them. I am the door. If anyone enters by

me, he will be saved, and will go in and out and find pasture. *The thief does not come except to steal, and to kill, and to destroy. I have come that they may have life, and that they may have it more abundantly.*
John 10:8-10 (NKJV)

So if Jesus said He came that I may have and enjoy life to its fullest extent, He was not going to leave any part of our lives untouched. We must allow Him to bring life, healing, and wholeness to everything that has died is unhealthy or broken in our lives for Him to fulfil His purpose in our lives. Anyone who has ever previously suffered lack in one of these five areas, and then experienced abundance later in their lives, will always tell you, *"I've had lack, and I've had abundance and abundance is always better."*

Being well in these five dimensions is better than being sick in your spirit, emotions, body, mind, or finances (yes, you can be unhealthy in your finances as well). Having your family intact and living in peace is better than having it shattered and in turmoil. Having more than enough money is better than having just enough or not enough. Living full of joy and peace is far better than living depressed, angry, sad (broken-hearted), or confused.

Jesus' Earthly Ministry Defined

"The Spirit of the Lord is upon me, because He has anointed me to preach the gospel to the poor; He has sent me to heal the brokenhearted, to proclaim liberty to the captives and recovery of sight to the blind, to set at liberty those who are oppressed; to proclaim the acceptable year of the Lord." Luke 4:18 (NKJV)

Jesus defined part of His earthly ministry (His mission statement) by quoting the prophet Isaiah 61:1-2a as recorded in Luke 4:18-21 (NKJV):

"The Spirit of the Lord is upon me, because He has anointed me to preach the gospel to the poor; He has sent me to heal the brokenhearted, to proclaim liberty to the captives and recovery of sight to the blind, to set at liberty those who are oppressed; to proclaim the acceptable year of the Lord." Then He closed the book, and gave it back to the attendant and sat down. And the eyes of all who were in the synagogue were fixed on Him. And He began to say to them, "Today this Scripture is fulfilled in your hearing."

From what Jesus said about His purpose and mission, we can conclude it was not only to bring salvation to humanity but also to heal us and to set us free from all kinds of bondage and oppression. *Jesus is not only concerned about our eternal life, but He is also profoundly interested in our lives here on earth.* Jesus demonstrated that through the many miracles, signs, and wonders He performed during His time on the planet. He also equipped and empowered men and women throughout the ages to do the same works He did. Jesus gave the mission to the church (the Body of Christ in the earth). It is through this "body" that He is fulfilling the mission the Father gave Him to do. Let us explore how Jesus'

ANDRE H. VAN ROOI

mission impacts these five dimensions of our lives.

SPIRITUAL DIMENSION

"The Spirit of God has made me; the breath of the Almighty gives me life" (Job 33:4, NIV).

Our spiritual redemption is the most crucial area of our lives. Without this dimension of our lives redeemed or intact, every other area of our lives will lack and be deficient and in the light of eternity, futile. There will be nagging in our hearts until this dimension is satisfied. We will try to fill that void with many things, but only what is genuinely spiritual can satisfy the spiritual hunger inside of every human heart.

To understand why this spiritual hunger and longing exists in the heart of man, we need to go to the book of beginnings (Genesis). We need to understand the origin of our spiritual dimension to receive the answer for which our hearts are longing. We need to know and understand why we feel so incomplete.

Man: Made In God's Image And Likeness

So God created man in his own image, in the image of God created he him; male and female created he them. Genesis 1:27 (KJV)

After God completed His work of creating the heavens and the earth and everything in it, He created man in His image and likeness. God designed humanity to be like Him, which probably accounts for the many religions that teach that we are all gods, and many others strive to be as a god. God wrote in our DNA; therefore, it is impossible to escape it:

> And God said, "Let us make man in our image, after our likeness: and let them have dominion over the fish of the sea, and over the fowl of the air, and over the cattle, and over all the earth, and over every creeping thing that creeps on the earth." So God created man in his own image, in the image of God created he him; male and female created he them. Genesis 1:26-27 (KJV)

> "And the LORD God formed man of the dust of the ground, and breathed into his nostrils the breath of life; and man became a living soul." Genesis 2:7 (KJV)

The man became a living (spirit) being after God "gave" him the breath (spirit) of life. The breath (life) that was in God was what gave man his spiritual life. It was what made him in the image and likeness of God. The body of a man can only live while his spirit is in him. When it departs, his physical life will also cease to exist, because the primary purpose of our body is to house the spirit of God. Through our bodies, we operate in the material/physical realm and through our spirits, we function in the spiritual realm: "The Spirit of God has made me; the breath of the Almighty gives me life" (Job 33:4, NIV).

Although we have physical bodies that will eventually perish, our spirit being is our real life. Our spirit being is the part of us that will live eternally, it can never die. The Apostle Paul reminds us that God's original intent for us was to be His children: *"The (Holy) Spirit himself testifies with our spirit that we are God's children"* (Romans 8:16, NIV).

Just as natural children have the traits and likeness of their parents, so were we created to have the characteristics and image of our Heavenly Father: *"Thus says God, the LORD, who created the heavens and stretched them out, who spread out the earth and what comes from it, who gives breath to the people on it and spirit to those who walk in it"* (Isaiah 42:5, ESV).

What Does God "Look" Like?

"God is a Spirit:" (John 4:24a, KJV).

We need to know what God "looks" like or is like, to understand what we were created to be or "look" like because He created us in His image and likeness. Jesus describes God this way: "God is a Spirit: and they that worship him must worship him in spirit and in truth" (John 4:24, KJV).

His children (creation) who received His breath of life, were given His nature and resemblance. Because God is a Spirit, and He created us to be like Him, we are of nature spirit beings. We can only relate to Him through our spirits. We will later explore how we use our physical bodies and soul (our will, mind, and emotions) in the expression of our spiritual worship of God, our Heavenly Father.

Separated From God: Lost Relationship With God

> *"You are free to eat from any tree in the garden; but you must not eat from the tree of the knowledge of good and evil, for when you eat from it you will certainly die." Genesis 2:17 (NIV)*

Adam and Eve had a living and vibrant relationship with God after their creation. God communed with them regularly. They had unlimited access to God. They were pure and holy, and God's sight. This identity, relationship, and access to God were, however, conditional; and they had to choose to either follow the life and prosperity or death and destruction that God had placed before them:

> Now the Lord God had planted a garden in the east, in Eden; and there he put the man he had formed. The Lord God made all kinds of trees grow out of the ground—trees that were pleasing to the eye and good for food. In the middle of the garden were the tree of life and the tree of the knowledge of good and evil.
> Genesis 2:8-9 (NIV)

> The Lord God took the man and put him in the Garden of Eden to work it and take care of it. And the Lord God commanded the man, "You are free to eat from any tree in the garden; but you must not eat from the tree of the knowledge of good and evil, for when you eat from it you will certainly die."
> Genesis 2:16-17 (NIV)

The story of God's relationship with man begins with Him giving humanity a free will. This free will meant that man could even use it to reject Him. *True love and meaningful relationship only come out of a free choice to love others.* It is no different in our relationship with God.

Genesis 3 details the decision of Adam and Eve to completely ignore God's command, which resulted in a lost relationship with God. Their lives were cursed, and God banished them from the perfect place He created for them, where they were supposed to live and commune with Him. This journey into darkness would last thousands of years, as the spirit of man cried out for the light and the life that once had in God:

> And the Lord God said, "The man has now become like one of us, knowing good and evil. He must not be allowed to reach out his hand and take also from the tree of life and eat, and live forever." So the Lord God banished him from the Garden of Eden to work the ground from which he had been taken. After he drove the man out, he placed on the east side of the Garden of Eden cherubim and a flaming sword flashing back and forth to guard the way to the tree of life. Genesis 2:22-24 (NIV)

The fatal decision to disobey what God commanded has led to untold misery, suffering, and pain for humanity. Man has now moved into the realm of "knowing" (experiencing) good and evil. Even today, humanity experience a tremendous amount of good and evil. God intended to spare us of the knowledge (experience) of evil. God designed humanity to live forever in the spiritual dimension. Adam and Eve lived for many years on the earth, in their physical bodies. They did not die physically (immediately), but spiritually toward God (Genesis 2:17). In this spiritual depravity and darkness, we've created and fashioned many humanmade gods and worshipped them in our attempt to recreate what was lost so long ago.

Reconciled To God: Regaining Our Spiritual Relationship To God

> *"Yet to all who did receive him, to those who believed in his name, he gave the right to become children of God—children born not of natural descent, nor of human decision or a husband's will, but born of God" (John 1:12-13, NIV).*

God did not forget about His children. His Son echoed his promise to redeem us: *"For God so loved the world that he gave his one and only Son, that whoever believes in him shall not perish but have eternal life" (John 3:16, NIV).* Eternal life was given initially to humanity in Genesis. This everlasting life was the timeless knowledge of God and being in relationship with Him. So, how does fallen humanity receive back what it lost in the Garden of Eden? Here is God's answer: "Yet to all who did receive him, to those who believed in his name, he gave the right to become children of God—children born not of natural descent, nor of human decision or a husband's will, but born of God" (John 1:12-13, NIV).

Jesus reiterated this truth of humanity regaining what was lost: Our spiritual relationship and identity with God. These things are resurrected (brought back to life, be born-again) by the power of God. As God placed His breath of life into man in the book of beginnings, He is again putting the breath of His Holy Spirit into man. He did this through the sacrifice of the life and the offering of the blood of Jesus Christ to pay for our sin and disobedience: "and without the shedding of blood there can be no remission of sins" (Hebrews 9:22b, NKJV).

Jesus said to Nicodemus:
Jesus replied, "Very truly I tell you, no one can see the kingdom of God unless they are born again." "How can someone

be born when they are old?" Nicodemus asked. "Surely they cannot enter a second time into their mother's womb to be born!" Jesus answered, "Very truly I tell you, no one can enter the kingdom of God unless they are born of water and the Spirit. Flesh gives birth to flesh, but the Spirit gives birth to spirit. You should not be surprised at my saying, 'You must be born again.'"
John 3:3-7 (NKJV)

What a marvellous truth revealed to humanity! If we would only believe and accept what God alone can do for us, we can receive the spiritual life/rebirth (connection to God) that we initially had when He created us: "And it is impossible to please God without faith. Anyone who wants to come to him must believe that God exists and that he rewards those who sincerely seek him" (Hebrews 11:6, NLT).

Humanity invented many substitutes, in our attempt to find a way back to God (and to be a part of the kingdom of God). Many even say there is more than one way to get to God and that every person has to find his way. I believed this for a good part of my life. I even attempted to encounter God through some of those other ways, but I had to be honest with myself eventually. All the ways I tried left me more lost, empty, depressed, and confused. Jesus answered the question once and for all. Many do not like or accept His answer, but here is what He said about the way to get to God: *"Jesus answered, 'I am the way and the truth and the life. No one comes to the Father except through me'"* (John 14:6, NIV).

So simple and yet so profound. *Only believe this simple truth.* That's it. No more, no less. Just receive the payment already received. A mystery of all mysteries and wonder of all wonders. Can it be all that simple? *Absolutely*. That is what His love has done for us. Can you even fathom a love like that? I still marvel at it today decades after I believed it and received the beautiful gift of God's salvation:

For God so loved the world that he gave his one and only

Son, that whoever believes in him shall not perish but have eternal life. For God did not send his Son into the world to condemn the world, but to save the world through him. Whoever believes in him is not condemned, but whoever does not believe stands condemned already because they have not believed in the name of God's one and only Son. John 3:16-18 (NIV)

I now see the kingdom of God so clearly. It was there all along, "hidden" from my view because the god of this world blinded my eyes to the truth of God's love and care for me (2 Corinthians 4:4). However, now that God removed the scales from my eyes and my heart, I can see the truth of God's Word. I found the spiritual abundance for which my heart longed, and I grow into it more and more as time passes. However, it will take me many more lifetimes to truly understand the spiritual dimension opened up to me through Jesus Christ.

My pastor loves to have us repeat this truth: *"I am a spirit, I live in a body, and I have a soul."* You are a spirit yearning for the reality of the God who created you.

The Holy Spirit: The Supernatural Gift To Mankind

> *"If you then, being evil, know how to give good gifts to your children, how much more will your heavenly Father give the Holy Spirit to those who ask Him?" (Luke 11:13, NASB)*

In addition to the beautiful gift of salvation given to us through the sacrifice of Jesus Christ, God, in His wisdom and knowledge, gave us the Holy Spirit to lead, teach, guide, and comfort us. When the disciples became troubled and afraid because the Lord talked about returning to the Father, Jesus comforted them with these words:

> All this I have spoken while still with you. But the Advocate, the Holy Spirit, whom the Father will send in my name, will teach you all things and will remind you of everything I have said to you. Peace I leave with you; my peace I give you. I do not give to you as the world gives. Do not let your hearts be troubled and do not be afraid.
> John 14:25-27 (NIV)

Jesus taught His disciples another valuable lesson of God's abundant spiritual provision for His children, in the gospel of Luke: "If you then, being evil, know how to give good gifts to your children, how much more will your heavenly Father give the Holy Spirit to those who ask Him?" (Luke 11:13, NASB)

The Holy Spirit is one of the most beautiful gifts given to us, as believers, to help us in our natural and spiritual journey through life. The Holy Spirit has taught me many beautiful lessons. He has guided me in many critical decisions I had to make regarding my life (see some of the ways He guided me regarding my finances in the Financial Abundance chapter).

The Holy Spirit: My Guide In Coming To America

I will instruct thee and teach thee in the way which thou shalt go: I will guide thee with mine eye. Psalm 32:8 KJV

When my wife and I decided to move from South Africa to the United States of America in 1989, I spent a lot of time praying and waiting upon the Lord to confirm it was the right decision for us as a family. We made all the necessary preparations to leave, but I was still waiting for that final confirmation from the Lord. As we packed some of our belongings one night, I heard the Spirit of the Lord speak to me as though He were right next to me. He told me, *"You are going to the United States."* Those words from Him sustained me through some of the toughest days of my life in my new country. I knew it was His will for us to be in the USA; therefore, I knew He would bring me through every trial and tribulation.

Imagine leaving everything that you've known and worked for your whole life, and starting over again in another country. We were about 8,000 miles away from friends, family, and our culture, with less than $2,000 in our pocket and expecting a baby. We had no furniture, no car, no family, no friends, just the belongings we could fit in our suitcases and a word from God, through His Holy Spirit. The Holy Spirit further enhances the abundance of the spiritual life that we so desperately need.

The Holy Spirit is the most precious comforter (companion) you will ever know. He brings the most beautiful and valuable peace into our lives like nothing or no one else can ever do for us. He has comforted me in so many ways and healed my brokenness so gently. He is tender, loving, gentle, and kind. He gently leads, guides, and teaches us the ways of the Father and moulds and shapes our hearts to be more and more like our Master and Savior, Jesus Christ.

The presence of the Holy Spirit in a believer's life is tangible and transferable. When the Holy Spirit of God fills you, you will know it. You will be able to transfer His presence to those you minister. I will not attempt to go into great detail about the work of the Holy Spirit because many men and women God has used mightily have written about the precious Holy Spirit in great length and detail. Among them are Dr Benny Hinn, Dr Kenneth E. Hagin, and many others whom God has significantly used since the beginning of the church. I would recommend you find out as much as you can about the Holy Spirit for your life and ministry. The Holy Spirit is the power needed to live a successful godly life and to be an effective witness and minister of the Gospel of Jesus Christ.

Jesus told His disciples to wait for the promise of the Holy Spirit before they launched out into the world. What a spectacular event it was (see Acts 2) and how wonderfully the Holy Spirit transformed those ordinary fishermen and other disciples into powerhouses for the gospel. They turned their worlds upside down through the power of the Holy Spirit working mightily in and through them on the earth.

You need only to invite the Holy Spirit into your life to have Him become your most magnificent companion. Ask the Father for the Holy Spirit, like a little child would ask of their father to provide them with sustenance for their daily life, and the Father will fulfil His promise of giving the Holy Spirit to you.

You can pray to the Father like this: "Father, you said in your Word that you would give the Holy Spirit to those who ask of you. Father, I desire the gift of the Holy Spirit, and so I ask you for the Holy Spirit according to Your Word, and I now receive the gift of the Holy Spirit from you, in Jesus' name" (Luke 11:13).

The Holy Spirit: My Comforter

And I will pray the Father, and he shall give you another Comforter, that he may abide with you for ever; John 14:16 KJV

I will relate one incident with you, where the Holy Spirit was such an incredible comfort to me (see more in the next chapter on the Emotional Dimension). One thing that was severely lacking in our family was tenderness and warmth. There were no hugs, kisses, or "I love you" in our family. I was a follower of Jesus Christ for about a year, and I remember having an emotional meltdown. I was an emotional basket case and a wounded and broken human being. My parents never uttered the words *"I love you"* to any of their children that I can remember. My mom, I know, loved us, but we never received much in terms of affirmation or encouragement.

I was home alone, in the place where we lived, and just had such a desperate need for unconditional love and acceptance. I wanted to know I was "okay" and worthy of being loved and just needed a hug. I am a huggy, touchy-feely kind of guy, and I just needed a hug to let me know that I was "okay." I sat on this big Papasan chair in our living room and wept my heart out. Then, ever so gently, there were gentle arms, wrapping themselves around me, and holding me so tenderly and securely. I knew it was the Holy Spirit, my comforter, who came in that time of my need to reassure me of the Father's love for me. There is nothing like the hug of the Holy Spirit to comfort and console you. What an awesome comforter and friend He is, able to touch us at the deepest point of our need. He has remained my strength, my com-

ANDRE H. VAN ROOI

forter, my teacher, and my guide.

EMOTIONAL DIMENSION

He heals the brokenhearted, binding up their wounds
Psalm 147:3

After I accepted the sacrifice Jesus made for my spiritual life and restored my relationship with God, I found I still had a tremendous amount of emotional baggage that I carried with me. I was a born again, Holy Spirit-filled child of God, on my way to heaven. However, I was still profoundly wounded and brokenhearted as a result of the abuse I endured as a child and the only son (I had three younger sisters) of an alcoholic father.

ANDRE H. VAN ROOI

Spiritually Restored But With A Broken Heart

My father was a broken man himself, and I don't know much about his life because he never talked about it. My dad did not speak much about anything to me my entire childhood. I know his father (my grandfather) died when my dad was around eight years old, and that was about as much as anyone has ever told me about my dad's childhood. My father medicated his brokenness and pain with alcohol, which added another "evil" dimension to his life. In addition to his brokenness, it resulted in more confusion and brokenness in our family. Broken hearts make for broken relationships and families.

My dad ended up spending money meant to take care of his family on alcohol. I remember many times when the rent and bills were left unpaid, and there was no food in the house. I remember times when my mom had to run for her life while protecting her family from my father's madness. I remember being woken up one night with my mom struggling with my dad at my bedside. He had a knife in his hand and was trying to stab me while I was asleep. I bore the brunt of his brokenness, pain, and confusion. There were many other abusive events I had to endure as a child that left deep scars in my heart. This pain did not become any easier to bear as I grew older. I was clinically depressed and did not even know it. My parent's marriage eventually fell apart, and they separated when I was seventeen years old.

Our brokenness passes on to the next generation, and they will likewise pass it on, continuing the cycle for generations to come. When our hearts remain broken, it allows the enemy of our souls an entry point in our lives. He will exploit any brokenness he can find in our lives. Broken heartedness is one of the main areas he will use to keep you bound, confused and lacking what God has already paid.

So many of us walk around with smiles on our faces, trying to mask the pain buried deep inside of us, but it will eventually manifest itself in our lives in ways that are not pleasant or constructive to ourselves or those around us.

He Came To Heal The Brokenhearted

"He heals the brokenhearted and binds up their wounds"
Psalm 147:3 (NIV)

Most human beings experience some form of emotional pain, brokenness, and distress. Not only were/are our spirits crushed and broken but so were/are our emotions/heart (some to a higher degree than others). The pain in our hearts is sometimes worse than the physical pain we experience in life. Through natural means and medicine, we can heal our physical wounds, but where is the cure for our broken hearts (the seat of our emotions)?

Medicine offers some relief, but, more often than not, it only covers (masks) the pain that is buried deep inside our broken hearts. It deals only with the symptoms of our brokenness, but not with the root cause of it. I'm not discounting what the field of psychology or medicine has accomplished; please understand me. Some relief is better than no relief at all. I have found, however, that too many times we are trying to heal our emotional wounds with medications, which is impossible to do. I would have diagnosed as a classic ADHD (Attention Deficit Hyperactive Disorder) kid growing up, but I was only acting out of the emotional turmoil of my life.

If we look at the mission statement of Jesus in Luke 4:16-19, we find that the healing of the brokenhearted (Luke 4:18) was the second assignment on His list: "The Spirit of the Lord *is* upon me, because He has anointed me to preach the gospel to the poor; *He has sent me to heal the brokenhearted,* to proclaim liberty to the captives and recovery of sight to the blind, To set at liberty those who are oppressed" (Luke 4:18, NKJV). God has always been concerned about the brokenhearted as has offered healing to us throughout the ages:

"The LORD is close to the brokenhearted and saves those

who are crushed in spirit" (Psalm 34:18, NIV)

"He heals the brokenhearted and binds up their wounds" (Psalm 147:3, NIV)

We know that God does not change. He is the same yesterday, today, and forever (Hebrews 13:8). It is time to take God at His Word and to experience abundance in your emotional life the way God intended you to have. It is time to receive healing. It is time to stop the enemy from having a foothold in your life. It is time to take back your life and everything the thief has stolen from you, killed, and anything he has destroyed in your life.

Keys to Start the Healing Process

"The Lord is compassionate and gracious, slow to anger, abounding in love. For as high as the heavens are above the earth, so great is his love for those who fear him." Psalm 103:8-9 KJV

Love: The Healing Balm

Love is the most excellent healing balm in the world. I know of no other godly attribute that can bring so much healing, peace, and contentment than the love of God and the love of other human beings. See what King David says in Psalm 103. He knew the love, compassion, and grace of God well: "The Lord is compassionate and gracious, slow to anger, abounding in love. For as high as the heavens are above the earth, so great is his love for those who fear him."

The Apostle John experienced the same love of God, as King David did. He recorded the words of Jesus for us: "For God loved the world so much that he gave his one and only Son, so that everyone who believes in him will not perish but have eternal life" (John 3:16, NLT).

> "So we have come to know and to believe the love that God has for us. God is love, and whoever abides in love abides in God, and God abides in him."
> 1 John 4:16 (ESV)

I believe it was the tremendous love and compassion people sensed flowing out of Jesus that drew the spiritually hungry, the broken in spirit, the brokenhearted, and the broken in body and mind to Him. Jesus' compassion caused Him to ignore an entire crowd to focus on two blind men.

Now as they went out of Jericho, a great multitude followed Him. And behold, two blind men sitting by the road, when they heard that Jesus was passing by, cried out, saying, "Have mercy on us, O Lord, Son of David!" Then the multitude warned them that they should be quiet; but they cried out all the more, saying, "Have mercy on us, O Lord, Son of David!" So Jesus stood still and called them, and said, "What do you want me to do for you?" They said to Him, "Lord that our eyes may be opened." So Jesus had compassion and touched their eyes. And immediately their eyes received sight, and they followed Him. Matthew 20:29-34 (NKJV)

Believe And Receive Healing

Just as I did not become broken overnight, my broken heart did not heal overnight. I wish the healing had been instantaneous because it feels so incredibly good to be whole. Just as healing of our physical bodies takes time after injury, even so, our broken hearts are mended over time if we accept and believe the fact that God wants to heal us, when we allow God him.

There is nothing you and I can do to deserve what God has for us through Jesus Christ. It was His great love for us that moved Him to pay the ultimate price: His death on the cross. There is no sin against any human or against God that is so great that His love cannot forgive. It is time to stop believing the lie that you are not good enough or that you've sinned way too much for God to forgive you. You can never disappoint God. King David says it so well: *"He has not dealt with us according to our sins, nor punished us according to our iniquities. For as the heavens are high above the earth, so great is His mercy toward those who fear Him; as far as the east is from the west, so far has He removed our transgressions from us"* (Psalm 103:10-12, NKJV).

Say this out loud: "Lord, I believe that you came to heal the brokenhearted of which I am one. I receive this healing for my broken heart right now. Thank you for healing me. Thank you for putting back together all the broken pieces of my heart."

Believing and receiving are two of the keys to receiving abundance in your emotional life. Unless you believe and receive what God has promised, you will always be on the outside looking in, wondering why others appear to be so happy and full of joy. He paid the price for all of us, not just for some of us.

Forgive Those Who've Sinned And Will Sin Against You

"Forgive people when they sin against you. If you do, your Father, who is in heaven will also forgive you. Matthew 6:14 NKJV

Another vital key to receiving your emotional healing is forgiving those who hurt (sin/sinned against) you. Jesus deals with this topic as recorded in the Gospels of Matthew, Mark, and Luke. "Forgive people when they sin against you. If you do, your Father, who is in heaven will also forgive you. But if you do not forgive people their sins, your Father will not forgive your sins" (Matthew 6:14-15, NKJV).

We must forgive others so we can be wholly healed of our brokenness and washed from our guilt and shame. I hear you saying, "But I thought I was forgiven of all my sins when I accepted Jesus Christ into my life." Yes, we were! We were born with a sin nature (see Romans 3:23, 5:12), and we need to be "born again" with a new "God nature." However, you might still be experiencing guilt, shame, brokenness and have bitterness in your hearts toward the people who sinned against you. Forgiveness liberates you from all of these conditions and breaks the strongholds the enemy might have over your life. Guilt, shame, bitterness, and unforgiveness rob you of the freedom and joy you should have and experience in Christ. It makes you feel unworthy, incomplete, almost dirty, and sometimes worthless and deserving of the burden that it brings into your life.

I experienced this freedom in my life as I forgave my earthly father and all his atrocities against my mom, my sisters, and me. I did not stop there. I forgave everyone I could remember who had sinned against me. There were many and what they did were grievous and shameful. *I was specific in my forgiveness toward everyone.* For example, I would say something like this: "I forgive my father for trying to stab me while I was asleep" and "I forgive my father for punching me in the chest so hard that I fell back about three feet and hit the wall." Even the hard and shameful ones that took me a long time to share with anyone, I forgave. I said, "Father (meaning God), I forgive [this person] for sexually abusing me when I was a boy, young and defenceless."

Whenever someone and something came to mind about some sin against me, I would immediately forgive that person for that specific sin. This forgiving others their trespasses against me went on for many years as the Lord brought people and events to my attention. The more I did it, the easier it became. Remember: *"being confident of this very thing, that he who began a good work in you will perfect it until the day of Jesus Christ"* (Philippians 1:6, ASV).

Once you break the bondages in your life, the freedom we have in Christ will begin to manifest in it. Forgiving others allows God to remove the demons of guilt and the shame from your life, opening the door for blessings to flow into it. So take a moment here to reflect and release (forgive) those who have sinned against you. Do it so that you can also enjoy the freedom from the guilt and the shame. Be specific in your forgiveness and don't give the enemy a foothold in your life any longer.

Forgive Yourself.

"God does not even remember our sins anymore. I will treat them with kindness, even though they are wicked. I will forget their sins." Hebrews 8:12 CEV

We often overlook the forgiveness of ourselves, and yet it is no less important than the other keys mentioned earlier. We are quick to forgive others, but we have a difficult time forgiving ourselves. A lot of unforgiveness toward ourselves comes from shame and remorse for the things we have done. We will beat ourselves up, and the enemy is eager to join in the beating. He is the accuser of the brethren. Sometimes we feel justified, in a morbid kind of way, in heaping all this guilt and shame on ourselves, and we think we deserve to feel bad (forever) for what we've done to others.

After I had been serving the God of our Lord and Savior Jesus Christ for about ten years, I still had a lot of remorse, guilt, and shame over my already forgiven sins. I remember listening to a song one day that dealt with forgiving ourselves when I heard the Holy Spirit speak to me as clear as day. He told me that I was willing to forgive everyone in my life that had sinned against me, but I have not been willing to forgive myself. It was a turning point in my life: a turning point toward the freedom and abundance I have in my emotional life that continues to this day.

"God does not even remember our sins anymore. I will treat them with kindness, even though they are wicked. I will forget their sins." Hebrews 8:12 CEV

"When the time comes, I will make an agreement with them. I will write my laws on their minds and hearts. Then I will forget about their sins and no longer remember their evil deeds." Hebrews 10:16-17 CEV

He wants us to do the same and not remember our sins anymore, so forgive yourself. It is God's gift to you as well as the salvation He purchased for you on the cross. He washed it all away with the blood of Jesus Christ. So we will do well to agree with God also not to remember our sins and our lawless deeds. The Apostle Paul reminds us several times that our shame has been done away with by the Lord: "Now hope does not disappoint, because the love of God has been poured out in our hearts by the Holy Spirit who was given to us" (Romans 5:5, NKJV).

"As it is written: 'Behold, I lay in Zion a stumbling stone and rock of offense, and whoever believes on Him will not be put to shame.'" Romans 9:33 (NKJV)

Scripture says, "The one who believes in him will never be put to shame" (Romans 10:11, NIRV).

So no more guilty stains and no more shame and remorse for the things from which God ransomed you. Remember, it is the goodness (and love) of God that leads us to repentance, not His severity (Romans 2:4). Take time to let the Words of the Lord sink deeply into your heart. There are doubtless many hurtful memories that will come up in your heart and mind. Some of them may be painful and difficult to face, but face them we must, for us to break the stronghold the enemy has had in our lives for so long. It is time for us to break the bondage in and over your life. Let God apply the healing balm of His love, mercy, and grace as it floods into your life and remains there continually.

MENTAL DIMENSION

He is our peace that have broken down every wall of seperation. Ephesians 2:14 NKJV

One of the first benefits I experienced when I accepted God's great gift of grace was a tremendous peace not only in my heart but also in my mind. What price can you put on having peace in your mind? You know what I am referring to if you know anyone who does not have a sound mind. An unsound mind is one that is incapable of functioning correctly and rationally. When I talk about a sound mind, I'm not talking about someone who has brain injuries or who is mentally disabled. I'm referring to someone who has all their rational mental faculties, but cannot focus, has constant thoughts of suicide, bad memories replaying over and over again, dyslexia (I was dyslexic), or depression.

He Is Our Prince Of Peace

> *"For unto us a Child is born, unto us a Son is given; and the government will be upon His shoulder. And His name will be called Wonderful, Counselor, Mighty God, Everlasting Father, Prince of Peace." Isaiah 9:6 (NKJV)*

When we accepted Jesus Christ as our Lord and Savior, the Bible says He came to live inside of us. The greater one comes to live inside of us, and greater is He that is in us than he that is the world (1 John 4:4). So if Jesus is living inside of us, He brings everything that He is along with Him. What an awesome truth! He lives in us to will and to do His good pleasure (Philippians 2:13). The Bible says He is the Prince of Peace. When you have the Prince of Peace living and ruling inside of you, you are a beneficiary of the kingdom that belongs to the Prince of Peace.

"For unto us a Child is born, unto us a Son is given; and the government will be upon His shoulder. And His name will be called Wonderful, Counselor, Mighty God, Everlasting Father, Prince of Peace." Isaiah 9:6 (NKJV)

Not only is He the Prince of peace, but also He is our peace. Do you realize He has left no stone unturned as it relates to our lives? Paul stated so clearly that He made provision for every area of our lives: "But now in Christ Jesus you who once were far off have been brought near by the blood of Christ. For He Himself is our peace, who has made both (Jew and Gentile) one, and has broken down the middle wall of separation" (Ephesians 2:13-14, NKJV).

God Gave Us A Sound Mind

"For God has not given us a spirit of fear, but of power and of love and of a sound mind" 2 Timothy 1:7 (NKJV).

As I was (and still am) learning and growing in my knowledge of God and His Word, I began to see that God has a lot to say about our minds. One of the things I learned is from the following verse: "For God has not given us a spirit of fear, but of power and of love and of a sound mind" (2 Timothy 1:7, NKJV).

I learned God had another incredible gift for me while I'm living here on the earth: a "sound mind". He gave us the gift of a mind that is uncluttered, unencumbered, and free of fear, turmoil, and constant worry. What a wonderful gift to have: a mind and life that is at peace and rest! Our Heavenly Father, the abundant life-giver, has given this precious gift to His children.

ANDRE H. VAN ROOI

Keep Your Mind Focused On God And His Word

"You will keep him in perfect peace, whose mind is stayed on you, because he trusts in you" Isaiah 26:3 (NKJV).

Anytime I have to deal with fear, worry, or anxiety, I remind myself that fear and worry do not come from God. The enemy of our souls' likes to divert our attention from God, and toward our shortcomings, weaknesses, mistakes and sins. This diversion causes us to focus on these negative emotions and thoughts.

The Word of God is quick and powerful. It enables us to overcome swiftly and mightily, as we proclaim it in our lives. Knowing, meditating (focusing on), and proclaiming God's Word is the way we keep our minds stayed (focused on Him). In doing so, we find God is the one that keeps us in perfect peace. (Parentheses added to the verse below to clarify and personalize it): "You (God) will keep *him (me)* in perfect peace, whose (when my) mind is stayed (focused) on you (God), because he (I) trusts in you (God)" (Isaiah 26:3, NKJV).

The media of television and the internet throws a constant barrage of images and words at us. If we are not careful, we find ourselves seduced and overtaken by these words and pictures. We indeed are what we eat. The same is true: we become what we feed through our eye and ear gates. These words and images have only one purpose: to persuade you to believe its message. So be careful what your mind is set upon because it will become the blueprint for your life. Become deliberate at setting your mind on heavenly things and not so much on earthly things:

"Set your mind on things above, not on things on the earth" Colossians 3:2 (NKJV)

Proclaim God's Word Concerning His Promises

They triumphed over him by the blood of the Lamb and by the word of their testimony; Revelation 12:11a (NIV).

I speak God's Word out loud in my life continually (you have to know the Word of God to proclaim it over your life). I remind the devil often of what Jesus has done for me. God has given us power over the enemy of our souls. You have to exercise this authority to be effective in every area of your life, especially over your mind. It is the one area the enemy will continuously attack: "I have given you authority to trample on snakes and scorpions and to overcome all the power of the enemy; nothing will harm you" (Luke 10:19, NIV).

You must remember there is a battle going on for your mind and your life. We overcome, by the "blood of the Lamb and the word (the speaking out) of our testimony" (Revelation 12:11). What testimony? The one about what God has done for us through Jesus Christ. The word about who you are in Jesus Christ, and who God is. Just like the devil wants to overcome you with his lies and deceit, so you must learn to subdue him with the powerful truth of God's Word (Sword of the Spirit). This sword is an offensive weapon, one to use to demolish the lies of the devil in every area of your life: "And take the helmet of salvation and the sword of the Spirit, which is the word of God" (Ephesians 6:17, NKJV).

Be Anxious For Nothing

"Do not be anxious about anything," Philippians 4:6a (NIV).

I have learned to trust God and the promises He made to us in His Word. I know He is not a man that He should lie (Numbers 23:19). So when He makes me a promise in His Word, I know He watches over His Word to perform it. I grab ahold of His promises, and I hold on to them for dear life. I can assure you, His Word is infallible and it works.

Believe it. Trust in it. Proclaim it. Stand upon it. Do battle with it.

If you do, He will set a guard over your heart and mind to protect it from anxiety. He does not want us to be anxious about anything: *"Do not be anxious about anything, but in every situation, by prayer and petition, with thanksgiving, present your requests to God. And the peace of God, which transcends all understanding, will guard your hearts and your minds in Christ Jesus"* (Philippians 4:6-7, NIV).

Don't Carry Your Burdens By Yourself

Cast all your anxiety on him because he cares for you" 1 Peter 5:7, (NIV).

I cannot tell you how many times I have prayed about issues, people, and situations in my life to be changed so that I could have peace. No sooner had I given them down to the Lord, then I would take them back again, to solve them through my efforts. A lot of times I did this out of frustration because sometimes God just "takes too long" to straighten things out. I felt like I needed to help him out just a little bit. The results of my effort were more frustration and strained relationships. Many times my pride would just get in the way of what God alone could do. I'm a slow learner sometimes, but He is helping me get better.

See what the Lord has to say about your cares. Not just the fact that He wants you to cast them on Him but look again, the verse says: He cares for (about) you and knows what your struggles and frustrations are, but He wants to do a work in you first before He takes care of all the stuff in your life: *"Humble yourselves, therefore, under God's mighty hand, that he may lift you up in due time. Cast all your anxiety on him because he cares for you"* (1 Peter 5:6-7, NIV).

You have to practice this whole concept of "casting all your care upon Him." It does not come naturally to most of us. Before we had Him in our lives, we had to make things work. We had to carry our cares by ourselves and what a burden that was. Thanks be to God who always causes us to triumph in His name.

So it does take humility to admit that we cannot carry our burdens on our own. We need a lot of help sometimes. His hand is mighty to save. Take Him at His Word. He already paid for your salvation with His blood, and He is offering to carry your burdens for you. It does not get any better than that. You have to believe He means what He says.

Renewing Our Minds

"Do not conform to the pattern of this world, but be transformed by the renewing of your mind. " Romans 12:1 (NIV).

One thing we can probably all agree on is this: as believers in the Lord Jesus Christ; we have to think entirely differently than the way we did before we got saved. The old mindsets, paradigms, and references are all challenged and need to be replaced by the "new" realities that exist in Christ.

I had to learn to forsake my thoughts and to begin thinking in line with those of God. I had to start agreeing with the Word of God. My thinking was unfruitful and destructive, and I was glad to get rid of them and to take on some new life-giving thoughts.

> Let the wicked forsake their ways and the unrighteous their thoughts. Let them turn to the Lord, and he will have mercy on them, and to our God, for he will freely pardon. "For my thoughts are not your thoughts, neither are your ways my ways," declares the Lord. "As the heavens are higher than the earth, so are my ways higher than your ways and my thoughts than your thoughts."
> Isaiah 55:7-9 (NIV)

Our minds can be a minefield filled with destructive thoughts and memories, just waiting for us to step on one so that it can blow up, and bring death and destruction into our lives. However, *we can "take back" our mind, and bring it under the control of the Holy Spirit through the Word of God.*

Through The Word of God, we learn what the mind

(thoughts) of God is. By planting the Word inside our hearts and minds, we'll begin to think like Him. His Word renews our minds, like nothing else in the world can do. His Word is spirit, and it is life (John 6:63); therefore, it will bring His life to us.

Renewing our minds will break the cycles of negativity in our lives and will give us new insights into our lives, and what God has made available to us. It will change the course of your life.

"Do not conform to the pattern of this world, but be transformed by the renewing of your mind. Then you will be able to test and approve what God's will is—his good, pleasing and perfect will" Romans 12:1-2 NIV.

"That ye put off concerning the former conversation the old man, which is corrupt according to the deceitful lusts; and be renewed in the spirit of your mind; and that ye put on the new man, which after God is created in righteousness and true holiness."
Ephesians 4:22-24 KJV

You have to remember that your mind is not "your" master. Your unfruitful thoughts should not define who you are. You are what the Word of God says you are. You are a child of God. The precious blood of Jesus Christ paid for you, and He desires that you become like Him: *"Let this mind be in you which was also in Christ Jesus, who, being in the form of God, did not consider it robbery to be equal with God" (Philippians 2:5-6, NKJV).*

There are countless books about the battles that go on for and in our minds. Suffice it to say: it is one of the critical components in the make-up of a human being. Whoever and whatever controls the mind of a person controls them.

You must take back control of what goes into your mind, and what your meditation will be. I like the saying: *You cannot stop the birds from flying over your head, but you can stop them from making a nest in it.* You (the eternal part of you, your spirit man, the real you) are the one that should be in charge. Your mind should be the servant to your spirit man and not the other way around. As your spirit man begins to grow and become stronger, it will start to have more dominance over the different areas (dimensions) of your life. In my book, "Extreme Mind Makeover: The God Edition", I address in more detail the process of renewing our minds.

Expel The Unfruitful Works Of Darkness

The fertile garden of our mind needs to be re-cultivated. We need to uproot the old things that take life away from us and re-plant the life-giving words and thoughts of God. It can and needs to happen if we are to live a fruitful life in God and His kingdom.

The fertile garden of our minds is re-cultivated when we begin to uproot and expel the unfruitful works of darkness from our lives, by slowly replacing it with the light of God's Word and His Spirit. Instead of death and destruction, bringing thoughts, we are admonished by the Lord to think differently than the way we did before. When we look at the list of things we need to think about, we realize we do have our work cut out for us:

> Finally, brothers and sisters, whatever is *true*, whatever is *noble*, whatever is *right*, whatever is *pure*, whatever is *lovely*, whatever is *admirable* — if anything is *excellent* or *praiseworthy* — think about such things. Whatever you have learned or received or heard from me, or seen in me — put it into practice. And the God of peace will be with you.
> Philippians 4:8-9 NIV

When you use the guideline set out in Philippians 4:8-9 to measure your thoughts, it becomes easier to recognize the unfruitful works of darkness in your life. Habits and ways of thinking do not happen overnight. Some things pass from generation to generation. We sometimes do not even question the validity or truth of these thought patterns. We sometimes blindly follow them, as if they are some sacred truth that would be sacrileges to examine or validate. It is therefore so important that we begin filling our hearts and minds, with the infallible and unchanging Word of God.

Destroy Thoughts Contrary To God's Word

I have said this before; however, it bears repeating: *Not all thoughts that come across your mind are yours.* Some ideas come from the enemy of our souls, who attempts (and succeeds many times) to convince us, that they are our own. It is good to remember that you are not the thoughts in your head. *You are what the Word of God says you are.*

So I can genuinely say many of these thoughts are illegal or criminal. You have to arrest them and take them into captivity. They should not be allowed the freedom to run around in our minds without being challenged. You must pull them down and throw them out.

> For though we live in the world, we do not wage war as the world does. The weapons we fight with are not the weapons of the world. On the contrary, they have divine power to demolish strongholds. We demolish arguments and every pretension that sets itself up against the knowledge of God, and *we take captive every thought to make it obedient to Christ.*
> 2 Corinthians 10:3-5 (NIV)

You arrest these thoughts with the truth of God's Word and proclaiming it over your life. You capture these thoughts by laying your hands on your head and applying the blood of Jesus to your mind. You should arrest fear, doubt, and unbelief when they assail your mind.

ANDRE H. VAN ROOI

Love God With Your Mind/Intellect

"Love the Lord your God with all your heart and with all your soul and with all your mind and with all your strength" (Mark 12:30, NIV).

Jesus emphasized the most important commandment God gave us. This commandment included instructions to love God with *all our mind or intellect:* "Love the Lord your God with all your heart and with all your soul and with all your mind and with all your strength" (Mark 12:30, NIV).

Why must we love God *with "all of our mind/intellect"*? I used to wonder just how I would go about doing this. I can understand loving God with my heart and soul, but to love Him with my mind/intellect—how do I do that? God does not expect us to "blindly" believe in Him, but He does want us to be prepared to answer anyone who asks, for the reason of the hope that we have (1 Peter 3:15). God does not require us as believers to put our brains "on the shelf" when we accept Jesus Christ as our Lord and Savior.

When I did not believe in the Gospel of Jesus Christ, I read and studied everything I could find contrary to the Gospel, so that I could prove God was not real, and that the Gospel was a fallacy. I studied to show myself approved in my ignorance of God. I found so many believers could not give me a reason for the hope they had in them. They do not study to show themselves approved, to rightly divide the word of truth (2 Timothy 2:15).

The world needs answers to the many problems it is facing. Jesus is the answer, but we need to be able to deliver the solution in a manner that the world can understand. The Apostle Paul was brilliant in his delivery of the reason for the hope that he had within him. We find in the Book of Acts (17:2; 18:4,19; 24:25) that Paul reasoned with people who needed a reason to believe in the message of the cross.

We might never attain to the level of Paul to reason with people, but we must endeavour to *engage our mind/intellect in the pursuit of the knowledge and understanding of God (Jeremiah 9:24)*. God wants us to know how He thinks, and why He does what He does. He wants us to know and understand Him with our mind/intellect. He wants us to love the truth of His Word, and His reasoning and actions. We do that with our minds as well as with our spirits.

I also believe loving God with our minds, is no different from loving God with the other parts of me. Love, even in the "natural" is consuming. It consumes our thoughts, time, and energy. Remember those days when you were in love and every waking moment (and many sleeping moments) you were thinking of being with that special someone. Our minds were preoccupied with love and devotion. People wrote some of the best poetry and songs when they are in love (I have even dabbled in a little love poetry myself). Being "in love" has led human beings to do crazy and extreme things for the sake of love (you might be one of those). It was God's love for us that caused Him to go to the extreme to prove His love for us.

So when He wants us to love Him with our minds, He wants our minds consumed with thoughts about Him. He wants our minds to be preoccupied with love and devotion for Him. God is not narcissistic; on the contrary, loving God with our minds is for our benefit and renewal.

Everything God commands us to do is for our renewal, enlightenment, and liberation. Loving Him with our minds brings freedom to explore everything that He has made available to us. A mind that loves God has access to God's mind and loves His Word, consumes His Word, meditates on His Word, and revels in His Word. *A mind that loves God is beautiful, indeed.*

As with everything else in our walk with God, we grow into it more and more as we give ourselves to the pursuit of God. If it is essential to God, it needs to be crucial to us. *Learn to love God with your mind/intellect.* Ask and allow His Holy Spirit to teach you His ways (our ways are not that great anyway). Let us grow more fully, and function more thoroughly, in the things our Heavenly Father has provided in His covenant with us.

PHYSICAL DIMENSION

He is the God Who Heals Us (Jehovah Rapha)

One of the covenant names of God is "Jehovah Rapha", which means "the God that heals" us. When you are in covenant with God, you are under the agreement of His promises. One of the fantastic promises we have from our Heavenly Father is that He is our healer.

> "He said, 'If you listen carefully to the Lord your God and do what is right in his eyes, if you pay attention to his commands and keep all his decrees, I will not bring on you any of the diseases I brought on the Egyptians, for I am the Lord, who heals you.'"
> Exodus 15:26 (NIV)

> "He heals the brokenhearted and binds up their wounds."
> Psalm 147:3 (NIV)

This covenant promise of God continued into the life of Jesus and His body, the church, in the earth today. If there is one particular thing that Jesus did that grabbed everyone's attention, then it must be the healing of people (*the deliverance of the demon-possessed; healing of the sick, disabled, diseased, lame, blind and deaf people*). It was one of the hallmarks of His ministry, and it caused people to pay attention to Him, and His message.

God's miracle-working power impacted whole countries (regions). People from all over Syria heard Jesus healed and set people free. They flocked to see the miracle-working Son of God.

> "Then His fame went throughout all Syria; and they brought to Him all sick people who were afflicted with various diseases and torments, and those who were demon-possessed, epileptics, and paralytics; and He healed them."
> Matthew 4:24 (NKJV)

Everywhere Jesus went, He displayed this one key attribute of God: our Healer.

> "And wherever he went—into villages, towns or countryside—they placed the sick in the marketplaces. They begged him to let them touch even the edge of his cloak, and all who touched it were healed."
> Mark 6:56 (NIV)

> "At sunset, the people brought to Jesus all who had various kinds of sickness, and laying his hands on each one, he healed them."
> Luke 4:40 (NIV)

There are thousands of reports of the same miracle power working through the church all over the world today. Believers around the globe who trust, believe and receive God's covenant promises are delivered and set free from the power of the devil. The church is the Body of Christ, and its purpose is to continue the work of the Lord in the earth today. We are not only to preach the Gospel of Salvation, but also to do the work that He did, and more significant works than what He did. It is another one of God's covenant promises, as recorded in the Gospel of John.

> "Very truly I tell you, whoever believes in me will do the works I have been doing, and they will do even greater things than these, because I am going to the Father."
> John 14:12 (NIV)

God is willing and more than able to keep His covenant promises toward us. Our job is to believe Him and to receive the promises He made to us.

It Is God's Will To Heal People

"'My food,'" said Jesus, 'is to do the will of him who sent me and to finish his work.'" John 4:34 (NIV)

Healing people was not a regular occurrence in the ministry of the Jewish priests or scholars when Jesus showed up. However, it has always been a part of God's covenant with His creation. God did not stop being Jehovah Rapha (the Lord our Healer) because He does not change. He is "the same yesterday, today, and forever" (Hebrews 13:8). Jesus and His disciples powerfully continued and demonstrated the ministry of healing throughout the last 2000 years. So when Jesus healed and ministered deliverance to people, *He continued the work of God the Father.* He was indeed doing the will of the Father, who sent Him:

> "For I have come down from heaven not to do my will, but to do the will of him who sent me."
> John 6:38 (NIV)

God has continued being *Jehovah Rapha*. Where the Word of God is declared and believed, it delivers what He promised. However, God's Word has no power or effect when rejected. In Mark 6, Jesus went to His hometown and taught on the Sabbath. Although people were amazed when they heard Him, they could not accept Him for who He was. They, therefore, did not believe anything He taught. They were even offended by Him.

> "He could not do any miracles there, except lay his hands on a few sick people and heal them. He was amazed at their lack of faith."
> Mark 6:5-6 (NIV)

How incredible is that? Their lack of faith limited the creator of the universe.

God Has Healed Me And Others

Let me tell you about one of the times God healed me. One day I sneezed so hard, it popped my sternum. It was a painful experience, and the pain did not go away. I remember driving to work one morning when a radiating heat came upon my sternum, and the pain left me entirely. It never returned. The memory of that moment is still fresh in my mind. I even remember to this day exactly where I was and when it was (I drove that route for about eighteen months between Irving and Forth Worth, Texas).

Then there was a time when I had acid reflux so badly I thought I had a heart attack. The symptoms were so bad, I checked myself into the ER. My heart was excellent, but it felt like a hole was burning in my stomach. That same night, we had the men from our church come together for prayer. I asked them to lay hands on me and pray for me. I was healed immediately. No medications, no more doctor visits, and none of the symptoms ever came back.

There were several other times when God healed one of my family members or me. I know people God has healed. There are several people that I have prayed for that God has healed. So to try to convince me that God does not do it anymore is futile. It is too late.

Some may argue by asking why God does not heal everybody we pray for who is sick. I don't know all the reasons why this happens. That is something they will have to take up with God. I cannot speak for God regarding that matter. What I know is that it is the will of God to heal us, and God has healed, is healing, and will still heal people in the ages to come.

The Gospel Includes The Good News Of God As Our Healer

We still preach salvation 2000 years after Jesus first came to proclaim it. People are committing their lives to the Lord in their multiplied millions all over the world. However, not everyone who hears the Gospel accepts it, but that has not stopped us from preaching the Gospel and believing and trusting in God or His Word.

We know from Scripture that God watches over His Word to perform it (Isaiah 55:11). My job is to believe God's Word and to act upon it, for me to see the results of it in my life.

That is what *the Gospel is: good news*. Good news to a sick person is that they can be made whole. Good news to someone who is in pain is that they can be set free from that pain. Good news to someone who is in bondage to addiction of a substance is that they can be delivered and be set free from those addictions. Good news to someone who is demon-possessed is that we can cast the demons out, and they can live free from its oppression.

What excellent news: it is God's will to heal us. Shout it in the face of the enemy:

My God is my healer.
My God is my deliverer.
My God is my redeemer.
My God wants me to heal me.
My God has already healed me.

By His Stripes, I Am Healed

> *"But he was wounded for our transgressions, he was bruised for our iniquities: the chastisement of our peace was upon him; and with his stripes we are healed."* Isaiah 53:5 (KJV)

When God spoke through the prophet Isaiah, about what Jesus would endure for us, He mentioned *healing as a specific benefit* of the severe punishment Jesus would suffer. The brutal mutilation of Jesus looked like defeat in the eyes of the world and the devil, but what a glorious victory it was for us.

> "But he was wounded for our transgressions, he was bruised for our iniquities: the chastisement of our peace was upon him; *and with his stripes we are healed."*
> Isaiah 53:5 (KJV)

The cure for our sickness and diseases was the mutilation of our Savior. His wounds and the stripes on His back are the remedy and payment for the infirmities of humanity. So if you are experiencing sickness, disease, pain, or any kind of physical affliction, you can *confidently and boldly declare* (and repeat) the Words of the Father: "With His [Jesus'] stripes, I am healed."

Regardless of the symptoms, outward appearance, or diagnosis, by His stripes, you are healed. Hearing what the Word of God says is believing, not seeing. The Word of God says faith comes to us by *hearing the Word* of God (Romans 10:17). *You must listen to the Word of God until it becomes a reality in your life.* Not wishful thinking, but unshakeable confidence (faith) in the truth of God's Word produces the evidence/substance/tangible things we confidently expect from God (Hebrews 11:1).

We should never lightly esteem what God did for us on the

cross at Calvary. To say God does not heal people anymore and that all miracles of healing stopped would be to discount the work done on the cross. It would make the suffering Jesus endured before, during, and after the cross futile and of no effect for the healing of our broken bodies. If the suffering of Jesus only brought us healing for a short period, what guarantee do we have that anything else He bled and died for was for eternity? Salvation would have been for a little while. Deliverance from demonic oppression would have been for a little while. We would have received peace from God for just a little while. It would have brought the removal of our guilt and shame for just a little while.

No, my brothers and sisters, the work on the cross at Calvary were complete and total. Abundant life means what it says. It means abundance in every area, which includes wholeness in our physical bodies. Thank you, Jesus! You don't have to be sick, diseased, paralyzed or in pain anymore. Thank you, Jesus! Thank you, Jesus, for freeing us from demonic oppression and possession. You need to declare this over and over for your life until it becomes a part of your DNA. Let His words live and breathe inside of you. Allow it to bring life inside of you that is needed for you to step into, what God has made available to us as His children.

Let His Words be the weapon with which you fight the fear, doubt, and unbelief that the devil tries to lay on you. Let it be the weapon that destroys the work of the devil against your life, and the life of your loved ones. Let the Blood of the Lamb and the word of your testimony cause you to overcome and be triumphant. Fight the good fight of faith. If God is for you, then who can be against you?

> "And they overcame him by the blood of the Lamb, and by the word of their testimony; and they loved not their lives unto the death."
> Revelation 12:11 (KJV)

Turn From Evil And Sin No More

Why do people get sick and remain sick? Many times, it has to do with sin and disobedience in their lives. This disobedience is either toward God and sin or God's Word. Many times, when Jesus healed people, He told them to stop sinning, or else they would get worse.

> "Afterward Jesus findeth him in the temple, and said unto him, 'Behold, thou art made whole: sin no more, lest a worse thing come unto thee.'"
> John 5:14 (KJV)

Sin is one of the many reasons why people get sick and remain sick. So if you have sin in your life, and you believe God will heal you, you need to confess your sin to God. Stop sinning, and your healing will remain. However, if God heals you and you keep sinning, it will be your fault if something worse comes upon you. The children of Israel were told by God on numerous occasions to follow His commandments and to obey His Word. God said one of the benefits of serving Him and not idols was He would remove sickness from them, and that they would live long lives. This promise made to His covenant people in the Old Testament book of Exodus is a promise to us, His New Covenant people, for today.

> "And ye shall serve the Lord your God, and he shall bless thy bread, and thy water; and I will take sickness away from the midst of thee."
> Exodus 23:25 (KJV)

> "Be not wise in thine own eyes: fear the Lord, and depart from evil. It shall be health to thy navel, and marrow to thy bones."
> Proverbs 3:7-8 (KJV)

It is not only God's intention to heal us from sickness and diseases, but He also wants us to live a long, full, and healthy life.

Because he hath set his love upon me, therefore will I deliver him: I will set him on high, because he hath known my name. He shall call upon me, and I will answer him: I will be with him in trouble; I will deliver him, and honour him. *With long life will I satisfy him, and shew him my salvation.*
Psalm 91:14-16 (KJV)

FINANCIAL DIMENSION

Money Does Matter to God

There is probably no other area in the church that stirs up as much dissension and conflict as the area of finances. It is also the area of greatest unfaithfulness in the church. Understandably so, our enemy, the devil, knows more about the power of money than most Christians. He understands, more than Christians do, how the lack of funds hinders the spreading of the Gospel and the establishment of the church in the earth. People know full well the power of money to build earthly kingdoms and empires, but they scarcely understand the power of money for the establishment of God's kingdom.

Consider this: God said if we cannot be faithful with unrighteous mammon, then we cannot be trusted with true riches that come from heaven and that are eternal (Luke 16:11). God determines the extent to which He can trust you with true heavenly riches based on how much He can trust you with worldly wealth, or as Jesus puts it, with unrighteous mammon.

Money is essential to God and one of the keys to your growth and authority in the kingdom of God for eternity. How you handle your money is also an excellent measurement of your attitude and relationship with God. *How you manage money does matter to God.*

Money Is A Matter Of Our Hearts

God admonished the nation of Israel, and even believers today, to take care of His house by bringing the *whole* tithe into the storehouse so that there may be provision (or food) in it. God gave the body of Christ the responsibility of supporting the church financially. In return, God promised we would receive blessings from Heaven (not money from Heaven, but spiritual benefits, which will lead to financial benefits on the earth) that we will not be able to contain (Malachi 3:10). So there is a practical aspect to the act of tithing: God's house has to be taken care of by His people, and I see no other way of how to do it other than through our tithes and offerings (God feels the same way).

However, before we get to the "blessings", we cannot contain," we see how God takes the nation of Israel to task over their unfaithfulness in tithing and offerings (Malachi 3:6-9). I want you *to pay close attention to why the Israelites did not tithe,* and robbing God from what belongs to Him (Leviticus 27:30). *The reason the people did not tithe is that they severed their relationship with God because of money*. So when God told them to return to Him, they wanted to know how they were to return to Him. God's reply was, and I am paraphrasing, *"Stop stealing from me and pay me what belongs to me, then I will know that I have your heart."* Their treasure was somewhere else (not with God and His house), and therefore, their hearts were not with God and His house either.

> "For where your treasure is, there your heart will be also."
> Luke 12:34 (NIV)

They performed all their religious duties, some even faithfully; however, they did not realize their hearts had drifted from God. The signs were there, but they did not recognize it. God had to point it out to them.

God Will Provide For You: Childlike Faith In South Africa

When I first heard the message of tithing (this was soon after I accepted Jesus as my Lord and Savior) in South Africa, I knew in my heart that it was something I had to do. I did not consult with anyone (not even my wife, who was not a believer at that time). I just started tithing. At first, my wife did not like the idea of me giving a tenth of my income to the church, but for some reason, she never strongly objected to it, as I kept doing it with every one of my paychecks. It was also during this time that we considered moving to the United States. I had to inform my employer (in South Africa) at that time that I considered relocating. I knew if I told them, they would let me go that same day, which they did, and it was a few months before we moved to the USA. I knew in my heart that God would take care of us, and to make a long story short, my new employer in the USA paid me (in dollars) for the time I was without work in South Africa when I got to the USA. The faith of new believers is sometimes astounding; they are willing to trust God implicitly.

ANDRE H. VAN ROOI

God Comes Through Again In The Usa

We arrived in the USA (Dallas, Texas) on June 26, 1990, and I started working almost immediately. It became apparent soon, however, that I did not make enough money. We were expecting our second daughter, a house to pay for in South Africa, and rent in our new country. We had no car or furniture for a few weeks and no family or friends to call upon for help. I was able to get a second job delivering newspapers, which meant I had to get up at three o'clock in the morning to make the deliveries, get back home at six, and then try to sleep for another hour. I was tired most of the time, but I felt I had to take care of my family, this was before I learnt about God being my source.

I approached my new employer about an increase in my salary. I was one of the most senior team members on my project, making as much money as less-experienced team members. However, they were not willing to give me an increase. Things started going downhill, and in early November 1990, about four months after arriving in the USA, I was without a job. I was relieved and concerned at the same time. Relieved because I was so tired and worried because I had no idea what my next step would be.

Two weeks went by without me being able to find another job. I was able to rest and recover during this time. Whatever little bit we had saved up ran out quickly, and in two weeks, and we did not have enough to meet all our obligations. We considered not tithing until I could find another job.

My wife and I were on the way home one day considering our financial options. I turned on the radio (it was on a Christian station), and whoever was on at that time was talking about tithing and trusting and believing God, no matter the circumstances. My wife and I looked at each other, and we knew the message was for us (I remember that incident like it was yesterday). God gave us the answer to the questions we had asked. So we paid our tithe, which left us with $20. I still did not have a job.

That Sunday night, we went to the evening service at our

church. We had a guest speaker who was a pastor in Mexico. He was raising money to buy a piece of land to construct his church building. People made pledges to help toward the purchase of the property. I heard the Lord tell me to pledge $500 toward the purchase of the land. I shared this with my wife, and she agreed we should do it. So we did. I had no idea how we were going to make good on it, but I had such a peace in my heart about it. I do believe a man is only as good as his word, and I fully intended to keep mine.

The next morning, I received a call from a friend of mine telling me he had a contracting opportunity for me. They hired that same day, and to top it off, paid me twice as much as my previous job. I made good on my pledge in about a month, and I was a happy man because my wife was a happy woman. That's how quickly God can work on our behalf if we trust Him.

I have many more stories I can tell you that speak of God's faithfulness toward me (those who are faithful to Him), but suffice it to say, He is committed to His word. He is not a man that He should lie (Numbers 23:19). He watches over every word He has spoken to see that it comes to pass (Isaiah 55:11).

The writer of Proverbs declares God's blessings make a person rich, and you will enjoy His riches without any sorrow accompanying it.

> "The blessing of the Lord makes rich, and he adds no sorrow with it."
> Proverbs 10:22 (ESV)

Financial Abundance Is God's Idea

There are some mindsets and abuses in the church that gave the message of God's abundant supply a lousy reputation. Immature and ignorant believers will take no notice of what God has to say. They would instead rely on misinformation, traditions, and fables about biblical finances and prosperity. Unscrupulous people will take advantage of naïve and immature believers and manipulate them into giving beyond what the Word and the Spirit of the Lord should be leading them to do. People feel pressured to do so because they don't want to appear out of line with God or His servants.

However, if you study the Word of God and understand the heart of God the Father, you will understand His desire for His children to have abundance in every area of our lives. Financial (material) abundance is not man's idea; it is God's idea (see Deuteronomy 30:9, Joel 2:23-25). He is an extravagant God and an abundant provider of everything His children need. *Ask God for wisdom in the area of money (finances)*, and He will give you the understanding you need. I can attest to this myself. I was pretty clueless about money. I did not know how to manage and use it wisely, and I had to go through the school of hard knocks in this area. It was easy to manipulate me in the field of giving because I love to give, but I did not always do it with wisdom and understanding of what God's Word has to say about sowing and reaping.

When I was instructed by the Holy Spirit to give abundantly above my tithes and offerings, it always resulted in abundant financial blessing in my life. When the Holy Spirit did not lead me, it led to mostly frustration and disillusionment. Please don't make all the mistakes yourself. Humble yourself and learn from others. Learn from God and His Word. For some people, handling and management finance are natural. For some of us (especially those who grew up poor), this area can be a tremendous challenge. Take heart though, the Holy Spirit, who is our teacher and helper, will lead us and guide us through this vital dimension of our lives that requires restoration and mastering for us to fulfil our destiny and the purpose for which God created us.

God makes it clear in His Word: He wants to bless His children in every dimension of their lives. The financial aspect is most definitely a significant area that God has promised abundance for His children.

ANDRE H. VAN ROOI

Financial Abundance: God's Covenant Promise

When we review the Old and New Covenants, we find abundant evidence regarding God's desire to bless His children financially and materially. There are hundreds of Scriptures where God promises to take care of His children. Yet, there are so many of His children who are conflicted about this area of their lives. Remember, our God is not stingy, or unable to make provision for His children. He is not like some of our earthly fathers who were unable or unwilling to take care of His children. He has an abundant supply of all we need for this life and for the generations which follow after us. Listen to God's promise to his children as part of the Old Covenant.

> "The Lord shall open unto thee his good treasure, the heaven to give the rain unto thy land in his season, and to bless all the work of thine hand: and thou shalt lend unto many nations, and thou shalt not borrow."
> Deuteronomy 28:12 (KJV)

When we view the New Covenant, it is made plain and simple: Jesus became poor so we might become rich. If you think the "riches" mentioned only refer to money, you are missing it. If you believe it does not apply to it, you are missing it as well. He is the abundant life-giver—remember.

> "For ye know the grace of our Lord Jesus Christ, that, *though he was rich*, yet *for your sakes he became poor,* that ye *through his poverty might be rich.*"
> 2 Corinthians 8:9 (KJV)

Some people with poverty mindsets will quote Jesus, saying, *"The poor you will always have among you"* (Matthew 26:11). That is true, but you can decide if will fall into that category. If you do, you will undoubtedly prove God's Word to be true. *"As a man thinks in his heart, so is he"* (Proverbs 23:7).

I was poor and knew the pain and disappointment of poverty. I see the effects of poverty all over the world. There is no joy, honor, humility, or glory in poverty. There is no future or freedom in it either. Even the poorest of poor hope and pray for a better tomorrow. They dream of a time without lack. The desire to have enough, and even more than enough, is written in the hearts of man. *It is God's way.*

Blessed To Be A Blessing To The World

The financial abundance that God wants to bestow on His children, however, is not only for us but so that we can be a blessing to the world in which we live. There is a job that has to be done by the church in the earth. To get the job done requires money. God knows this, but some believers still have to grab ahold of this fact. God has already made provision for the things He expects or requires for His people. His body is supposed to be a blessing to the nations of the world. It is a challenge to be a blessing to the world around us when we have just enough or barely enough for our own needs.

It is interesting to note that although Mother Teresa took a vow of poverty, she still relied on the generosity and support of those who had money to accomplish her mission. Those who were blessed financially were able to be a blessing to Mother Teresa and her ministry. Even if she believed in God to provide all of her needs, God still did most if not all of the supplying of needs through people.

The church has been instrumental in many countries around the world to build schools, universities, hospitals, and to provide the basic needs to countless millions of people (welfare is the churches responsibility). Schools like Harvard and Yale were founded and influenced by those in the church that saw the need to educate God's people not only in our faith, but also in other vital areas of life such as business, politics, medicine, and science. Godly men and women recognized the role of the church in the earth. They knew the church is supposed to be a blessing to the world.

We cannot accomplish any of this, nor can we "lend unto many nations" if we don't have an abundance (Deuteronomy 28:12). Dr Oral Roberts, who founded Oral Roberts University (ORU), went through a significant financial crisis and was in danger of losing the university. God spoke to a wealthy businessperson who came to Dr Robert's aid and rescued the institution from financial ruin.

Hopefully, I have made my point: to be a blessing to others; we need to have more than enough to meet our needs. We need to have an abundant supply of financial resources to be a blessing to the world.

God's Part And Our Part In Financial Abundance

We have to be careful, however, not to view our paying of tithes and the giving of offerings to the Lord and His church as a *spiritual lottery*. Many believers treat it that way because they misunderstand God's intent regarding giving and receiving. They think they just need to pay their tithes and give offerings, and then God will somehow magically enrich them. They neglect to apply sound biblical and financial principles in the handling of their money, and then they expect God to bless their ignorance.

Before I appear too harsh, let me add that I am sharing out of my own life experience. I call it the *"ouch factor."* My ignorance and lack of wisdom hurt financially and emotionally. So let the pain of others be your gain. Do not let the apparent faith you have for finances negate the need for wisdom regarding your finances. Your "ouch" factor might become significant.

Be Shrewd About Money (Use Wisdom)

Let's look at an odd story that Jesus taught about money. I say "odd" because it appears as though Jesus is encouraging wrong behaviour. He is trying to teach a principle, not only about survival but how to operate in this world, as it relates to money (instead of waiting on God to do everything for you like opening up the windows of Heaven and pouring out a blessing that you cannot contain).

In *Luke 16:1-9*, Jesus tells the story about a person (steward) who worked for someone in a trusted position and was wasting his master's possessions. His master wanted an account of what he was doing and informed him that he could no longer be his steward. The steward went to some of the people who owed his master money and cut a deal with them by reducing the debt they owed to his master. These people get rid of money they owed, the master got money back on some (probably bad) debt owed to him, and the steward finds favour with people. They would more than likely help him out since he no longer had a job. The master commended the steward for being shrewd.

Jesus then made this statement at the end of Luke 16 as a *"pay attention"* moment: "For the children of this world are in their generation wiser than the children of light. And I say unto you, 'Make to yourselves friends of the mammon of unrighteousness; that, when ye fail, they may receive you into everlasting habitations'" (vv. 8-9).

I like the way the Message Bible puts it:

> Now here's a surprise: The master praised the crooked manager! And why? Because he knew how to look after himself. Streetwise people are smarter in this regard than law-abiding citizens. They are on constant alert, looking for angles, surviving by their wits. I want you to be smart in the same way—but for what is right—using every adversity to stimulate you to creative survival, to concentrate your attention

on the bare essentials, so you'll live, really live, and not complacently just get by on good behavior.
Luke 16:8-9 (MSG)

A lot of believers are complacent about their financial welfare and are shocked when they are in dire straits when their source of money or income dries. In the story above, the Lord is clearly stating the mindset we should have about and toward it. Being shrewd about money is not a sin. Understanding how the world works is not sinful. A wise and faithful steward understands even the master expects a return on his investment. Let's look at another well-known story out of the book of Proverbs regarding the management of income:

> *Go to the ant,* thou sluggard; consider her ways, *and be wise*: Which having no guide, overseer, or ruler, *provideth her meat in the summer,* and *gathereth her food in the harvest.* How long wilt thou sleep, O sluggard? When wilt thou arise out of thy sleep? Yet a little sleep, a little slumber, a little folding of the hands to sleep: So shall thy poverty come as one that travelleth, and thy want as an armed man.
> Proverbs 6:6-11 (KJV)

In both of these examples, God is giving us some wisdom, insight, and advice to the proper attitudes we should have in our financial affairs. The Lord is handing the church an indictment in the book of Luke when He tells us that the children of the world are wiser than the children of the kingdom when it comes to money: how to make it, how to hustle for it and maximize opportunities when it comes around. God's children stand around and wonder (and sometimes complain) that the world has all the money, and they are always struggling. They will rationalize away lack by spiritualizing their unwillingness to learn about and understand how money works. Many unsaved people do a lot of good with the money they have.

Having money and lots of it is not sinful. *Loving* money is what is the root of all evil. It is when money owns you that it becomes your master. Someone said, *"Money is a great servant but a terrible master."* The love (god) of money *will replace* the love we should have for God. So it is wise to understand this, but to no extent shy away from it completely. God will give you the grace and wisdom on how to master money if you allow Him to teach you from His Word and lead you by His Holy Spirit on how to manage money. The story of the ant is one of saving and storing up when things are going well (summertime) and not about consuming everything that we earn (like the locust) and having nothing for the winter times.

You cannot get into debt up to your eyeballs on purpose for stuff you don't need and then think you can have faith for God to get you out of debt. Nor can you "give" yourself out of the mess you've created in your financial life. God will have grace for us for a season, but when that season is over, He will allow us to learn from our mistakes.

Follow The Holy Spirit For Your Financial Well-being

In Romans 8:14, God teaches an essential principle regarding our walk with the Lord. It says, *"Those that are led by the Spirit of God, they are the sons of God."* Jesus said the Holy Spirit would lead and guide us, teach and counsel us. We need His leading and guidance, teaching and counsel in every area of our lives, but especially in regards to our finances and how we make it and not lose it. If there is one area of your life that will make you or break you, then it is this area of finances. *Money answers everything (Ecclesiastes 10:19).*

Let me tell you about a time the Holy Spirit "led" me. I was considering a new position in a company for which I worked. The job was in a different department from the one I was in at the time. The opportunity sounded exciting and promising. I spoke to the director of that department about it, and she was excited and open to having me on her team. I was eager and willing to take the opportunity as well. It seemed like a perfect fit for me. My wife and I both agreed I should take a new position. As I dressed to go to work one morning, after I spent my quiet time with the Lord, the Holy Spirit told me not to take the job. The director was in another country, and I was going to travel there a week or so later. When I got to see her again, I thanked her for the opportunity but told her that it was not an opportunity I wanted to pursue at the moment. I did not tell her any more than that, and she did not question me. Less than a month later, the company shut down that entire department and let everyone go, including the director. Many of these people struggled to find work again, and I might have been one of them if I had not paid attention to the Holy Spirit.

Do I always listen and follow the counsel of the Holy Spirit? Unfortunately not, but after suffering the consequences a couple of times, I endeavour to seek His counsel about every significant financial decision my wife and I make. *You have to develop the habit of asking the Lord how to use your money.* It is not easy making the transition to being led by the Holy Spirit, because for the most part, we might have it covered; however, I know even in my life, I can do better in how I spend and allocate my money. Invite the Holy Spirit to be your financial partner and take time to listen and follow His leading and promptings for your economic life.

Follow The Word Of God Regarding Your Finances

The Holy Spirit brings the Word of God to life for us. Without the illumination of the Holy Spirit, the Word of God can remain a mystery to us. It is a mystery to many believers. Jesus told His disciples that the Holy Spirit would bring to their remembrance everything He taught them and everything He did. We are the recipients of the revelation poured out by the Holy Spirit, through the writers of the Bible. They spoke and wrote the Word for us, as the Holy Spirit gave them revelation and utterance.

If you do not stray beyond the Word, you will be safe. However, you need to know the Word of God to understand what the Holy Spirit taught. The Word of God has a lot to say about money. It is one area that is covered in great detail because it is such a key area of our existence. God left us with more than enough instruction, guidance, and even warnings about money and the pursuit and handling of it. So none of us has any excuse, other than the fact that we never read or know what the Bible says and teaches us about money. Even if we know what the Bible teaches about money, we are not faithful or diligent to follow its instructions.

Tithes And Offerings

So what does the Word of God teach us about tithes and offerings? First of all, it teaches us to pay God a tenth (tithe) of our income and then it instructs to give offerings above our tithe. The offering is at our discretion, but the tithe belongs to God and is not negotiable. It is a straightforward plan God instituted for the maintenance of His "house" (temple). In paying our tithes and giving offerings, we empower the Word of God to go to all the nations. It is also a place where people could come and meet corporately to celebrate God. Churches are focal points in our communities and are a beachhead for the kingdom of God to be established in the earth. God-ordained it from the first tabernacle God asked Moses to build. Although God now dwells within us, He uses the local body and their facilities to bring attention to His work in the earth. His church is not supposed to be in hiding, even though it has suffered severe persecution throughout the ages.

Final Thoughts Regarding Finances

I know I have merely touched the tip of the iceberg when it comes to money. My desire was only to introduce you to the fact that God has your financial restoration and wellbeing at heart. We know His thoughts are not our thoughts and our ways are not His ways. *For as high as the heavens are above the earth so His ways are higher than our ways and His thoughts than our thoughts (Isaiah 55:7-9).*

I conclude this chapter by encouraging you to seek God regarding your finances. Seek His wisdom, will, and direction for this dimension of your life. Seek knowledge and counsel from others about your finances. Even if you do not have what you consider to be much, be faithful with what you have. Become a student and learn what you need to know about money. If you are like me, it is probably easier to just let someone else do it; but believe me, you need to stay on top of this area of your life, or else it will bring ruin you. If you are married and your spouse handles all the money affairs, get engaged and stay engaged in your finances. If you are single, find someone to whom you can be accountable. At least know what is coming in and what is going out. *Know the condition of your flocks and give careful attention to your herds (Proverbs 27:23).* Above all else, pray. Pray diligently and fervently for this dimension of your life.

YOUR TURN

Let the wicked change their ways and banish the very thought of doing wrong. Let them turn to the LORD that he may have mercy on them. Yes, turn to our God, for he will forgive generously. Isaiah 55:7 NLT

If what I have written in this book resonates in your heart, would you open your heart and mind to the life-giving truth found in God's Word? If you have not done so before, would you like me, acknowledge your desire and need to know this unconditional love and mercy? Are your life without meaning and lasting purpose? Is there a cry of desperation in your heart for meaning and fulfilment? Are you wounded, broken, and empty?

Jesus is able and will change your life if you embrace what He has done for you. Your response to receiving all that God has for you is so simple that many people miss it. There are no hoops to jump through, no mountains to climb. Good works cannot earn you His love. The only response required from you is to say: "Yes Jesus, I need you. I need you to help me answer the cry of my heart. I accept what you did for me on the cross. I accept that you died on the cross for me. I accept that you died for my sins. Forgive me of my sins. I thank you that you died that I may have life and have it more abundantly. Come into my life, Jesus, and be my saviour, my Lord, and my master. I will follow you, Lord, wherever you may lead. Take my life and make it worthwhile."

That is the most fantastic response that anyone can ever give to the tremendous gift of love and eternal life that God has given us through Jesus Christ. There is no other name given under Heaven that saves man, and that name is "Jesus Christ" (Acts 4:12).

If you have prayed and sincerely meant that prayer, *"For it is with the heart that you believe and are justified, and it is with the mouth that you profess and are saved" (Romans 10:10, NKJV).*

You are now in God's family. Everything that Heaven has is now available to you forever. Welcome to the incredible journey you will ever take in your life. Welcome to God's family! Your life will never be the same again. Our journey into the abundant life that God has for us starts with us receiving the gift of God's abundant mercy and grace with sincerity of heart and intent. It is the first step that every person has to take to make this journey meaningful and significant.

Start this journey. Put on your walking shoes, and let's live this abundant life that God has for us.

FINAL WORDS

The journey to restoration and abundance in these five dimensions of our lives is just that: a journey. It must be walked out, worked out, fought and prayed for. It takes time and patience to allow God to work in these five dimensions of our lives. If we let Him, God will restore every one of these dimensions to places of abundance and fruitfulness in our lives and into the lives of those we get to touch. There undoubtedly will be times of great victory, setbacks, obstacles, seeming defeat, and pain in the journey. However, if we persevere and remain faithful in your pursuit of God, He will not leave any area of your life untouched.

Trust Him, believe Him, and obey Him, and your life will be a fruitful and well-tended garden that will produce a bountiful harvest for the kingdom of God.

Your brother in Jesus Christ and servant to all.

ABOUT THE AUTHOR

    I was born and raised in one of the most beautiful cities in the world (I'm a little biased), Cape Town, South Africa. As a child, we were a part of a denominational church, where my family attended for generations. As my family fell apart during my teenage years, I became disillusioned with what I thought I knew Christianity to be. Through my Kung Fu teacher, I learned about Buddhism, which sounded more appealing to me than Christianity. I subsequently became a follower of that religion and studied it for about ten years.

    I, however, found myself so empty and without joy and peace in my life. I began to question the reason and purpose for my life. At the age of twenty-seven, I decided to reach out to God (whoever He was) and asked Him to make Himself known to me. I told God that if He is real, it should not be difficult for Him to let a mere man, like me, know He is real. At that moment, I felt a burden lifted off my life, and it began my pursuit of this God who answered my prayer so quickly.

    Where before I shunned the Gospel of Jesus Christ, I now found myself intently listening to it whenever people preached or read it out loud. I loved to hear people worship God, even if I did not participate. Over four months of gently wooing me, I was "caught" by the fisher of men, and became His disciple and have been serving Him faithfully ever since January 1990. There is no one like Him in all the earth; no one who can save, deliver and heal as He does. What an incredible saviour and God He is. Over the years, God has used using me effectively to minister healing and deliverance to His children in these five areas of life as believers in Jesus Christ.

BOOKS BY THIS AUTHOR

Living A Christ-Centered Supernatural Life

Are you looking for more in your Christian Faith, other than what has become so routine, and maybe even dull and boring? Fact of the matter is, our life in Christ is supposed to take us into the supernatural world that Jesus talked about and demonstrated so powerfully. This has been the intent of God, for us to live beyond the natural world, because we are supernatural beings. In this book we will discover what gives us access to the supernatural world, and how we can live in it, as a normal part of our Christian life.

Extreme Mind Makeover: The God Edition

One of the crucial and most often overlooked areas in our Chrstian lives, is the renewing of our minds. We focus mostly on our spirit, emotions, and our physical bodies. However, if we do not transform our minds, we will always live a limited life in God. In this book you will discover how much God has to say about our heart and mind, and He gives us complete instructions on how to transform them.

Printed in Great Britain
by Amazon